WWW.MAXINE.COM

Published by Hallmark Books,
a division of Hallmark Cards, Inc.,
Kansas City, MO 64141
Visit us on the Web at Hallmark.com.

Editors: Bill Moses and Emily Osborn
Art Director: Kevin Swanson
Creator and Illustrator: John Wagner
Designer: Mary Eakin
Contributing Designer: Jack Pullan
Production Designer: Bryan Ring
Special thanks to: Jack Pullan, Amanda Raymundo,
Nancy Fulton, and Stephanie Allen

ISBN: 978-1-59530-309-7
BOK2104

Printed and bound in China

Hallmark
gift books

Agin' and Ragin'!
Maxine Older, Wiser, and Just Generally More Annoying!

DEAR MAXINE FAN,

Sometimes I get asked how old Maxine is. For obvious reasons, I don't like to answer this question. Maxine has true fans of all ages, so to some degree, I think she's however old you want her to be. And also … I've seen firsthand what she does to people who talk about her age.

That said, right now I feel compelled to talk about Maxine's age anyway … and just this once, I don't think she'll mind. That's because this year marks the 25th anniversary of Maxine's first appearance on a Shoebox card. Just imagine all the scorn she's heaped on deserving victims in those 25 years! Imagine the army of grousers, malcontents, and incorrigible sourpusses she's prodded and provoked!! Imagine the number of file folders I have to keep track of!!!

OK, sorry … I got a little off topic there. My point is that in her own grumpy way, Maxine has changed the world … maybe even for the better! I, for one, can't remember a time when we more desperately needed a voice that could cut through all the crap and just plain tell it like it is.

I'm not saying that Maxine's is the only voice out there that can stand up to the craziness we see around us every day. And I know for a fact that Maxine wouldn't say that either. She would say that all the Maxine fans out there are just as capable of yelling it like it is as she is, and she would be right. (Trust me, I've seen the fan mail.)

And there's one other thing she would say on this occasion (besides, "Time to shut up and draw something, Arty Boy"): She would say A GREAT BIG, CRABBY THANK-YOU to all the fans who have joined her on her 25-year journey. And as her #1 fan, I think I could speak for all of us by saying, "Thanks for the memories, Maxine. And here's to your next 25 years."

Keep on crabbin',

JWagner

John "Arty Boy" Wagner

Part one:
OLDER

Getting older is a pain in the butt. And the hip. And the knees. And the back. OK, you get the idea. Luckily, there's something we can do about it ... COMPLAIN! Share our ailments in excruciating detail! And once we've put the fear of aging into the people we love, we can rest easy knowing that the real secret of aging is safe ... the secret that it's actually not so bad.

There's a name for men
who find me fascinating ...
PALEONTOLOGISTS!

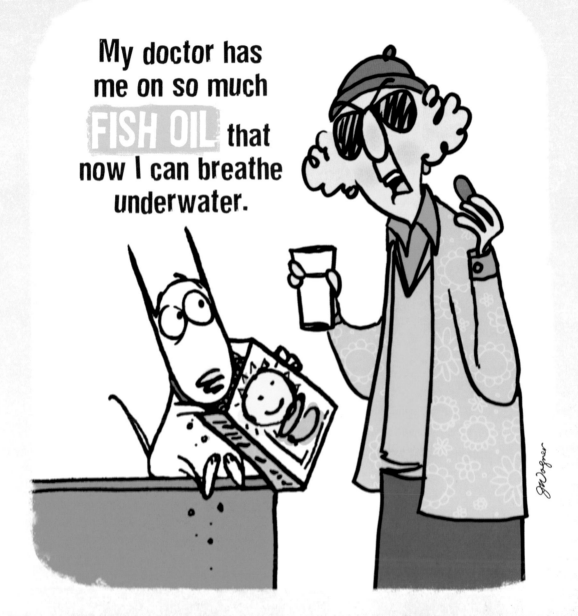

I wanted to get a **TATTOO** on a part of my body that wouldn't sag ... hence, no tattoo.

I'm no stranger to **PROTEST MOVEMENTS.** I have one pretty much every time I get up in the middle of the night to go to the bathroom.

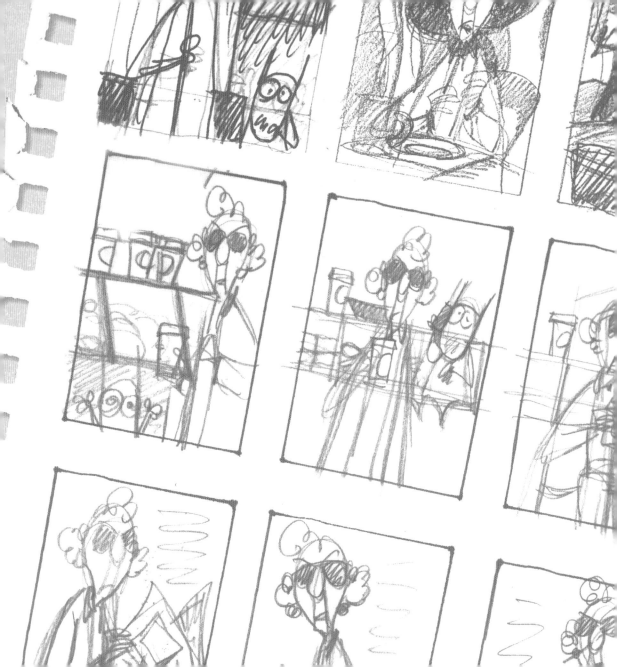

Part two:
WISER

They say that with age comes wisdom, but they never seem to say what's so great about wisdom. Well, I'm here to tell you ... with wisdom comes the ability to convince people that whatever you say is profound. But don't just take my word for it ... turn the page and be prepared to believe everything you read!

When people say they're AGING like a fine wine, they usually mean that their contents have settled to the bottom.

"**HANG IN THERE,**" people tell me.

Heck, I'm hangin' everywhere!

The older I get, the more I appreciate good lighting. The **OFF SWITCH** usually does the trick.

When you've seen as many years as I have, **LOSING YOUR MEMORY** somehow seems less bad.

I keep my
savings tucked
SAFELY AWAY
where nobody will
find it ... my bra!

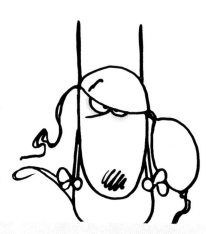

Part three:
MORE ANNOYING

You only really annoy the ones you love ... but don't worry, we can work on that. There are hundreds, maybe even thousands, of opportunities each day to be your pest ... ahem, I mean best. Everyone, from the cashier at the grocery store to the mailman, is a potential target. And one more tip: Don't bother trying to figure out why they deserve your petty wrath ... even if you don't know why, chances are they do!

If you have enjoyed this book
or it has touched your life in some way,
we would love to hear from you.

Please send your comments to:
Hallmark Book Feedback
P.O. Box 419034
Mail Drop 215
Kansas City, MO 64141

Or e-mail us at:
booknotes@hallmark.com